True Tales of Trying Times

Legal Fables for Today

PROFESSOR BOB RAINS

Illustrated by
E. A. Jacobsen

With a foreword by
Justice J. Michael Eakin
Pennsylvania Supreme Court

Willow Crossing Press LLC

Wildy, Simmonds & Hill Publishing Ltd.

PUBLISHED BY
Wildy, Simmonds & Hill Publishing Ltd.
58 Carey Street, London WC2A 2JB England
AND BY
Willow Crossing Press LLC
355 East Baltimore Street, Carlisle, PA 17013, USA
www.willowcrossingpress.com

Text © 2007 by Robert E. Rains
Illustrations © 2007 by E.A. Jacobsen
All rights reserved

10 9 8 7 6 5 4 3 2 1

ISBN: 978-1-898029-90-8 (UK edition)
ISBN: 978-0-9793686-0-8 (US edition)

Library of Congress Cataloging-in-Publication Data
Rains, Bob, 1949-
True Tales of Trying Times: Legal Fables for Today
Illustrated
Includes Foreword by Justice J. Michael Eakin
p.   cm.
1. Humor—Law. 2. Legal humor. 3. Fables.
PN6231.R13
813.54 R13   2007924805

Designed, edited, and typeset by Rodelinde Graphic Design
Printed in the United Kingdom by Cambridge University Press

Contents

On the Road

Love and War

Animal Farm

Order in the Court

Workers of the World

Rights of Way

All in the Family

Crime and Punishment

Holiday Stories

Foreword

Once upon a time in the vineyards of the law, there toiled a man who aspired to help those who would make fine wine from the study of cases that grew there. He helped his apprentices reap the large principles, and the small nuances too, and all the variations that lay between. To help these pupils become lawyers and counselors and advocates, he would illuminate legal doctrine and illustrate the human consequences. In doing this he enabled all to understand the majesty that is the law, and to appreciate the towering intellectual scholarship of the appellate courts.

But for all the happiness this brought him, from time to time he saw that not all cases dealt with matters of great weight. The bulk of the harvest was not Marbury v. Madison,* but more likely involved Mrs.

---

* In case you don't recollect the episode from high school civics, Marbury v. Madison was the 1803 case in which the great Federalist Chief Justice John

---

Marbury v. Mr. Marbury. He saw that many cases did not lend themselves to opinions that would become pillars of jurisprudence. He noticed tales most odd, strange weavings of facts and persons unbelievable, with courts left to resolve matters more peculiar than scholarly. Then one day he saw a fable. He scarcely recognized it at first; indeed, he was not sure what he had seen. But not long after, he saw another. Then another, and soon he saw fables everywhere. There, amongst the cases most profound, were cases quite petty, nearly inconsequential, but clearly they were cases, and if you looked at them just right, they were indeed what he thought they were: fables waiting to be told. And he gathered them and now decants them for us all. And the wine is sweet and quite palatable. It is well worth the drinking.

A fable, says Webster's, is a fictional story used to demonstrate "a useful truth or precept." Bob Rains sees them. He helps us see them as they should be seen. Technically, these may not be fables, for they are

---

Marshall ruled that the Supreme Court has the power to declare laws unconstitutional even though the Constitution doesn't say so anywhere. Marshall figured that the Framers just plumb forgot this minor detail when they were drafting the Constitution. In honor of this judicial pulling-a-rabbit-out-of-a-hat, the leading organization today advocating judicial restraint and "strict construction" of the Constitution is named, you guessed it: the Federalist Society. [B.R.]

---

not fictional. But certainly they should be, for fact is indeed stranger than fiction. And just as some people tell jokes well and others can't, not everyone can recognize, much less narrate a fable. Bob Rains can, and here, does. And does well.

Although it has been said that the law is only "common sense, as modified by the legislature," such an aphorism only covers the statutes. To be comprehensive, some have added "and as misinterpreted by the courts," ensuring the case law is explained as well. The cases here may or may not belie this, but they certainly reflect the predicaments and quandaries the human species creates and throws upon the legal system. They are spawned by every circumstance and motive from the avaricious to the eleemosynary, and they reflect the resourceful endeavors of lawyers and the system to deal with them.

In a profession ruled by precedent, these stories all have value, if only as examples of what not to do. Their true worth, however, would lie unappreciated until described by the proper reporter. The teller of these tales makes them come alive, and displays their useful truths and precepts for all of us to appreciate. It is as though he reverses another fable, putting the clothes back on the Emperor, letting us see the cases not as bare trivialities, but as finery we would otherwise miss. As with so much of our education the teacher makes the lesson memorable and hence valuable. Bob Rains gives us lessons worth learning, with fables as broad as the fruited plain, and as addictive as salted peanuts. I defy the reader to read just one. Enjoy them all.

> Litigants and their counselors had best be chary
> when suing for matters so extraordinary
> that not only have they lost their case,
> they've earned the right to take their place
> as protagonists in the professor's anthology
> having gone to court for tripe, sans apology.
> It's been going on since Hector was a pup
> and heaven knows you can't make this stuff up;
> So read them all if you are able
> and learn from the master of the modern legal fable.

Justice J. Michael Eakin
Pennsylvania Supreme Court

Disclaimer

Discerning readers (and, we hope, book buyers) —

You hold in your hands True Tales of Trying Times, a collection of factual legal fables, actual stories of actual cases of men, women, and children, and sometimes even lesser life-forms, appearing in our judicial system, seeking (and sometimes seeking to avoid) that most elusive lady, Lady Justice. I did not invent any of these cases. There is simply no need to invent folly in the law; folly is there in abundance.

For the benefit of the English-speaking public, I have attempted to avoid all unnecessary legal jargon. While some of my colleagues may be disappointed, I have eschewed references to all the stuff we lawyers love (and charge for), such as mandamus, quantum meruit, and the Rule in Shelley's Case (whatever that may be). For those who, for some inexplicable reason, prefer to read the unvarnished truth, I have provided citations to all the cases in this little tome.

Attention attorneys and cite checkers: If you do read the cases cited and conclude that I have fudged a little here or slipped up a little there, please don't bring it to my attention. Either keep it to yourself, or write your own book.

Law students and would-be law students: While the legal wisdom of decades is contained in this slim volume, reading it is not, unfortunately, a realistic substitute for attending three years of law school. Your author is a law professor by trade and would be drummed out of the union were it otherwise.

Everyone else: Please enjoy these scribblings for what they are. Take them, like the truth, in small doses. And, whatever you do, stay out of court.

Bob Rains
Carlisle, Pennsylvania

Forewarning

Discerning readers, here's the gist:
Webster's says a "fabulist"
Is a person who is able
To concoct a clever fable,
Someone we might all admire
Were he not as well a liar.

ON THE ROAD

Guy and the Stud

Once upon a time in the land of Indiana, there lived a doll named Brenna Guy whose erratic driving came to the attention of a certain Officer Shaffer. This fine member of the constabulary directed Ms. Guy to pull her car over and gave her three field sobriety tests. Guy flunked them, one, two, three. The kindly officer asked Guy if she would take a chemical breath test, and, being a nice Guy, she agreed. Following oral protocol, Officer Shaffer examined the inside of Guy's mouth for foreign substances. All he found were a tongue and a tongue stud. Without further ado, he gave Guy the breathalyzer test, and, true to form, she flunked.

On appeal, the court agreed with Guy that a tongue stud, no matter where manufactured, is a foreign substance which must be removed so as not to taint breathalyzer results. Ergo, the blown breathalyzer had to be suppressed.

Moral:
Whatever women think of men,
A stud is handy now and then.

Two Cars
and One Cell Phone

Terry was driving down the street one spring day when her car was struck by a car being driven by Kellie. Kellie was allegedly (as we lawyers like to say) chatting on her cell phone at the time that her car attempted to occupy the same space as Terry's.

Knowing a deep pocket when he saw one, Terry's lawyer promptly sued the purveyors of the offending cell phone. He argued that the cell phone people were negligent as they knew, or ought to have known, that their customers would use their cell phones while operating motor vehicles. The trial judge, who was later affirmed on appeal, did to the lawsuit what Kellie should have done with her cell phone: threw it out.

Terry's lawyer was outraged to have been thus shown the door, and filed a motion to reopen the case based on newly discovered evidence. That evidence, duly submitted to the court, was a cartoon strip depicting the cartoon character Blondie talking on a cartoon cell phone while driving her cartoon car and causing a cartoon accident. Unimpressed by the probative value of this new evidence, the judge would not budge. The cell phone case remained disconnected.

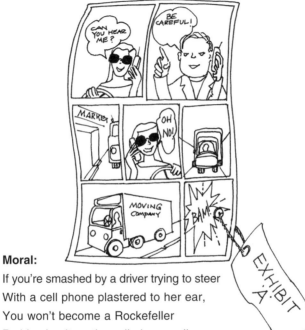

Moral:

If you're smashed by a driver trying to steer
With a cell phone plastered to her ear,
You won't become a Rockefeller
By blaming it on the cell phone seller.
And, should you file a cartoon strip,
The court will still award you zip.

The Pedestrians Who Tried to Make a Mountain out of a Molehill

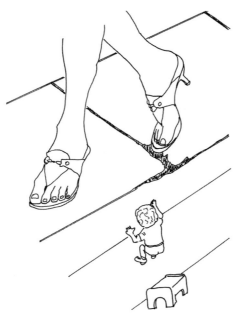

One fine day, Joseph and Josephine were innocently strolling along the sidewalk in front of Larry's house. Josephine was looking straight ahead when she tripped over a crack in the pavement, fell down, and hurt herself. Being modern Americans, Joseph and Josephine sued Larry for damages. The Js presented evidence of elevation differences in the offending sidewalk reaching an altitude of seven-sixteenths of an inch, a full three-sixteenths of an inch above the standard established by some very knowledgeable standards setters. Unimpressed by the enormity of the situation, the trial court found that the defect was trivial, letting Larry the homeowner off the legal hook.

The Js asked higher judges to review this admittedly pedestrian controversy. Those learned ones got out their magnifying glasses to examine the claim. After much weighing and measuring of the facts, they ultimately concluded that the plaintiffs' case simply was not what it was cracked up to be.

Moral:
If you don't watch where you are going,
The law won't find a duty owing
Should you step upon a crack
And wind up lying on your back.

The Driver
Who Rested His Case

Tim had been driving since three o'clock in the morning and was dead tired. Around one in the afternoon, his truck was observed traveling in the wrong lane of traffic. A nearby driver saw that Tim was asleep behind the wheel. Shortly thereafter, Tim's truck struck a motorcyclist and severely injured her.

At first, Tim was contrite. He approached the motorcyclist and said, "What have I done?" By the time the police arrived, however, Tim had come to his senses. In a show of paternal loyalty, he told the cops that his sixteen-year-old son Joshua had been behind the wheel when the accident occurred. Unfortunately for Tim, but fortunately for Josh, there were just too many of those pesky eyewitnesses for the cops to buy that story.

By the time Tim went to trial on charges of criminal recklessness and false informing, he was wide awake to the dangers he faced. The jury, who probably thought that Tim was a bad dad as well as a bad driver, convicted him of all charges. Less contrite than ever, Tim directed his legal dream team to file an appeal.

As you know, appellate judges are always alert to a potential miscarriage of justice. No doubt the judges reviewing Tim's case ordered in lots of lattes to enable them to stay up late, poring over tomes filled with legal wisdom. Quickly concluding that Tim had given false information to the investigating officers, they affirmed that conviction.

Turning to the criminal recklessness count, the judges weren't so sure. They recognized that Tim had fallen asleep at the wheel in the middle of the day, driven on the wrong side of the road, and collided with a motor-cyclist, causing her great harm. But, was all this sufficient evidence of reck-lessness? The state hadn't proved that Tim consciously ignored warnings that he was tired and might fall asleep. Because Tim wasn't conscious when he crashed, he hadn't made a conscious decision not to be con-scious, so the judges found he wasn't criminally reckless.

Moral:

The law says do not drink and drive, so you and others may survive.

But if by chance you drive and snooze, your driver's license you won't lose.

The Passenger
Who Tried to Pass the Buck

Brian and Stephen had themselves a night out on the town, partaking in that time-honored tradition known as barhopping. They downed a few drinks at Salivar's Bar and a few more at the West Cove. By the time they departed the West Cove, they were definitely feeling no pain. Alas, that situation was not to continue. With Stephen behind the wheel, the happy celebrants got into a one-car accident, and Brian was injured.

Stephen was convicted of drunk driving. Perceiving a potential silver lining, Brian got in gear and sued. . . Salivar's and the West Cove. Brian claimed the accident was their fault because they continued to serve Steven drinks when he was already well lubricated. But wait, the bar owners responded, it was you, Mr. Big Shot Brian, who purchased a lot of those rounds and then slipped into the passenger seat.

Sadly for Brian, the courts sided with the saloons. While the judges surely admired Brian's generous spirit, they concluded that one who springs for spirits for his driver should not be heard to complain when that driver drives drunk and none too well.

Moral:

If you make like a big spender
And treat your driver to a bender,
You can't expect to score some cash
When you are injured in a crash.

Sitting Duck

Robert was feeling all tuckered out, so he sat down to relax and take a load off. Any doctor would advise you that this is a sound course of action when your body tells you it's time to take a rest.

But even a good idea may be poorly executed, and this one was. Robert might have chosen more wisely his place of repose. Perhaps his judgment was impaired by the substantial amounts of alcohol he had consumed. Perhaps the alcohol added to his feelings of fatigue.

For whatever reason, Robert sat his weary bones down upon the tracks of the New York City Subway System. This was fine until a subway train came along; then it wasn't fine. In the collision of train and Robert, the train won. Miraculously, though, Robert came out alive, if somewhat the worse for wear.

Seeking to reverse his fortunes, Robert sued the New York City Transit Authority. He claimed that the train operator had been negligent in not stopping for a customer who chose to repose upon the train tracks.

But Robert was no more successful in his legal battle with the Transit Authority than he had been in his physical battle with one of its trains. The courts concluded that it was Robert's reckless conduct in

choosing his resting place, which he was lucky was not his final one, that caused his injuries, not the negligence of the conductor for having had the audacity to drive the train on its tracks.

Moral:
If you feel tired and unfit
And wish to pause and rest a spell,
It's not a great idea to sit
Upon a subway track, or el.

The Driver Who Had
an Open-and-Shut Case

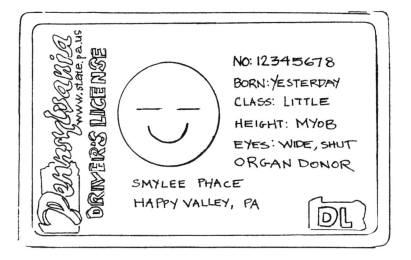

When it was time for Billy to get his driver's license renewed, he dutifully betook himself to the photo license center in Reading, Pennsylvania, and had his driver's license photo taken. The driver's license photo taker noticed that in the photo she had taken of Billy, his eyes were shut. This will not do, she told Billy, you can't have your eyes shut on your driver's license photo. You need to have the photo retaken, this time with your eyes open. Billy's appeal to her supervisor was unavailing. The supervisor informed Billy that the License Technician Operations Manual requires that the photo on your license have your eyes open. Billy refused, and left with his pride intact, but no new license.

Billy took his case to a Department of Transportation hearing officer. Billy lost. Billy took his case to the Pennsylvania Secretary of Transportation. Billy lost. Without the wise counsel of an attorney, Billy appealed to the Commonwealth Court of Pennsylvania.

Billy argued that his First Amendment right to freedom of expression had been violated because a photo is an expression of himself. He claimed that his right to happiness was also violated because it would make him happy to have his eyes closed on his driver's license photo.

The judges of the Commonwealth Court did not see eye to eye with Billy. You must be dreaming, said the judges. Wake up and look around you. If you were as good a pupil of the law as you think you are, you would see that your claims are frivolous. The constitution doesn't guarantee a citizen the right to do whatever makes him happy, and opening your eyes is a small price to pay for a driver's license. In an effort to cheer Billy up, however, the judges did quote a famous philosopher who warned, "The search for happiness is one of the greatest sources of unhappiness."

They might have added that when you're searching for happiness, just as when you're driving, it's best to do so with your eyes open.

Moral:

When dealing with bureaucracy,

It may seem arbitrary, but

The wisest course that I can see

Is to keep your eyes open and your big mouth shut.

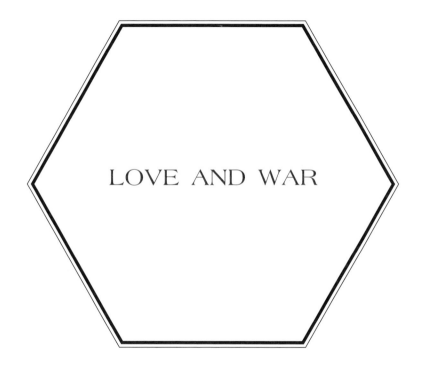

LOVE AND WAR

A Man and a Woman

In the County of Suffolk in the Commonwealth of Massachusetts, there lived a woman who wanted to have a baby and a man who wanted to have sex. The man had four children by a prior marriage, and the woman had none. The man said that the woman should not worry because a fortune-teller had told him that he would have six children. So the man and the woman did have sex, but no new children arrived. After several months of having sex, the man remembered that he had forgotten to tell the woman that he had also had a vasectomy. But, nothing ventured nothing gained, they kept having sex anyway, until one day the man found someone else. This made the woman mad and she stopped having sex with him. Then the woman sued the man for all sorts of legal misdeeds, such as infliction of emotional distress and fraud and battery, for not having told her about his vasectomy in the beginning. After all, he knew her biological clock was ticking.

The court was, of course, shocked – shocked! – that a man might say, or not say, things to a woman in a deceitful manner to try to get her to have sex with him, but reluctantly concluded that such matters are beyond the expertise and jurisdiction of our legal system.

Moral:
Choose well with whom you copulate
If you intend to populate;
For even if you raise a squawk,
The law won't punish pillow talk.

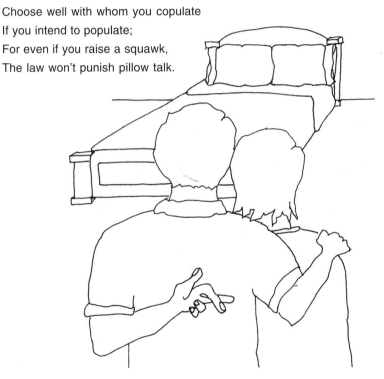

The Artist, the Artiste, and the Attorneys

Once upon a time, an artist and an artiste got married. They shouldn't have. He was a famous American sculptor. She was from Hungary, but had achieved fame in Italy performing in a certain type of movie which does not have a wardrobe budget. They had a son. They shouldn't have.

After love departed, the artist and the artiste engaged in a really big international custody battle over their pride and joy. In late 1993, the artist flew the lad out of Italy, conveniently ignoring an Italian court order directing him not to do so. Back in New York, the artist got an order from the New York courts in early 1994 prohibiting the artiste from taking the kid back. Of course, within a few months, the artiste managed to lift the kid.

The artist hired a topnotch New York law firm to "leave no stone unturned" in the ongoing custody battle. His attorneys left no stone unturned. They called the State Department, the Ambassador, and the Congress. With extreme diligence, they even watched many of those wardrobeless movies, no doubt searching for evidence.

Despite their heroic efforts, the attorneys were unable to get the artist back his son. They were, however, able to generate legal fees of just under $4 million. The artist only paid them a paltry $2 million, which made his attorneys awfully angry. So they sued him.

The artist hired still more attorneys to defend himself against the first attorneys. The artist argued that the first attorneys' fee was excessive and unenforceable. He got some expert witnesses to opine that a $4 million legal fee is a bit much for a custody dispute.

The judge, no doubt once an attorney himself, disagreed. He concluded that a court should "not police the conduct of wealthy litigants who choose to share their wealth with counsel through extravagant litigation."

Moral:
A life in the law can be mighty fulfilling
Once you have mastered the fine art of billing.
Why, even if clients should greet it with scorn,
You can charge them top dollar
     for studying porn.

"Honey, I have to
work late again tonight."

A Nice Round Sum

The only thing worse than having to pay your own lawyer is being forced to pay your ex-wife's lawyer who has just beaten you up in court. Anyway, that's how Michael felt when a generous judge ordered him to pay $1,000 to Kenneth Tarlton, Esq., who had represented Michael's wife Deborah in the untying of the knot.

Payment was due on November 1, so on October 30 Michael had his agents deliver the $1,000 to Attorney Tarlton's office in nice round pennies, 100,000 of them, unrolled, in twenty bank bags.

Attorney Tarlton researched the matter and found a bank which redeemed the 100,000 pennies for a $100 fee, thus netting him only $900. A precise fellow, Attorney Tarlton also calculated that it took him 2.7496 hours to collect and redeem the pennies.

Attorneys like to be paid for their time and effort. So, in the next round of litigation, Michael was sued not by Deborah, but by Attorney Tarlton, for the bank's $100 redemption fee, $350 in attorney fees and $83 in court costs.

The courts found that Michael's penny payment plan was frivolous and ridiculous, and ordered him to pay Attorney Tarlton the money he sought for his time and losses. But this time the judges took no chances. In the event that Michael didn't pay by cashier's check or money order, still preferring cash, he was ordered to fork over exactly five $100 bills, one $20 bill, and three $1 bills, no more, no less.

Moral:

Attorneys cost a pretty penny,
But if you pay them with too many,
They'll likely think that isn't nice
And you may wind up paying twice.

The Husband
Who Lacked Imagination

Robert and Judith were married and had a daughter, but alas they did not live happily ever after. After a quarter-century of togetherness, they opted for apartness. In the divorce settlement, Robert promised to pay Judith $750 per month in alimony, which could be terminated if Judith started cohabiting with a male.

After several years of shelling out Judith's severance pay, Robert asked the court to let him off the hook. The problem, he said, was not that Judith had taken up with another man. Rather, after the divorce, Judith had decided to make other changes in her life. Notably, she had undergone a sex change operation and had become a male. Not only was Robert still paying alimony to his ex-wife, who was now an ex-female, but to add insult to injury, the ex-Judith had taken up with a girlfriend. In a sense, Robert found himself compelled to fund the competition, and he didn't like it very much.

Too bad, said the court. We've reviewed your divorce settlement very carefully, and it just doesn't cover this eventuality. You should have thought of this before.

Moral:

When true love turns out to be phony

And you're facing alimony,

Make sure the settlement protects

Your wallet if one day your ex

Her own anatomy rejects.

Or you might have to subsidize

More than you might realize.

The Very Patient Mistress

When Gail first met David, he was less than forthcoming with her. He led her to believe that he was divorced, which was not precisely the case. The two became lovers, but Gail soon discovered that David was still encumbered with a wife. So David told Gail that he had moved out of the marital residence in order to get a divorce. Somewhat mollified, Gail stuck with David, who just happened to be rich as sin.

Over the years, David provided Gail with some very good goodies. He paid her rent on various homes, took her for trips around the world, bought her fancy trinkets, and allowed her, in the court's words, "the use of his luxury yachts." (Your humble reporter is not aware of any other type of yacht, but perhaps doesn't travel in the right circles to know of such things.)

Apparently David's divorce was a particularly protracted one. The years turned into decades. Although it would appear that David's marriage was not exactly made in heaven, he did continue off and on to live with his wife.

Some twenty-three years into David's relationship with Gail, he told her it was all over. Gail was devastated, so devastated that she went to a psychiatrist and a lawyer. The psychiatrist told her she was devastated. The lawyer sued David on Gail's behalf.

Gail claimed that she had only remained with David because of his frequent promises to divorce his wife, marry Gail, and support her for life. He should be held to his promises of permanent support, she said.

Sadly for Gail, the court didn't see things her way. In order for the law to enforce a promise, the promisee must have reasonably relied upon it. While the court was not exactly clear as to when Gail's reliance became unreasonable, it concluded that she should have gotten the big picture in somewhat less than two decades.

Moral:

A lass who waits for twenty years,
For Romeo to leave his wife
Is bound to wind up veiled in tears
Despite her beau's domestic strife;
And our courts will greet with jeers
His promise of support for life.

The Wife Who Shrank and Disappeared

When Clyde's marriage to Marylynne fell apart, so did he. Clyde was so distressed that he didn't know what to do. To try to relieve his pain, Clyde got himself a lawyer and sued... Marylynne's therapist, Dr. V.

Clyde claimed that his marital woes were all Dr. V's fault. Dr V had treated Marylynne before and during the marriage. Dr. V should have known that Marylynne couldn't keep the marriage commitment, but still encouraged Marylynne to give it the old college try. Dr. V had continued to encourage Marylynne to patch things up with Clyde even after Clyde had dropped a rather big hint that he had had it with her unwifely behavior by suing her for divorce. Clyde argued that Dr. V had a duty to warn him before the wedding that the fair Marylynne was just not marriage material. Clyde sought damages from Dr. V for intentional infliction of emotional distress and professional negligence. Husbanding her resources, Dr. V got her own lawyer to defend her professional honor and private assets.

The trial judge did to Clyde what Clyde had done to Marylynne: rejected him. Seeking to find more sympathetic ears, Clyde appealed.

While the judges of the Superior Court are surely superior to trial court judges, nevertheless they sided with this particular trial judge on this one. They reviewed the legal standard for intentional infliction of emotional distress, and found that to collect damages against Dr. V, Clyde would have to show that Dr. V had engaged in atrocious conduct utterly intolerable in a civilized society. Past cases included examples like killing someone's kid and hiding the body. Dr. V may have been a trifle optimistic in encouraging the Clyde-Marylynne nuptials – even outrageously optimistic – but this just didn't meet the test for atrocious conduct.

Turning to the negligence claim, the Superior Court recognized that a psychologist does have a duty to warn an intended victim of a patient's specific and immediate threat of serious bodily injury. But, unfortunately for Clyde's appeal, serious bodily injury just does not include a broken heart.

Moral:
If your dear wife should break your heart,
No matter what you think
It really isn't very smart
To try to sue her shrink.

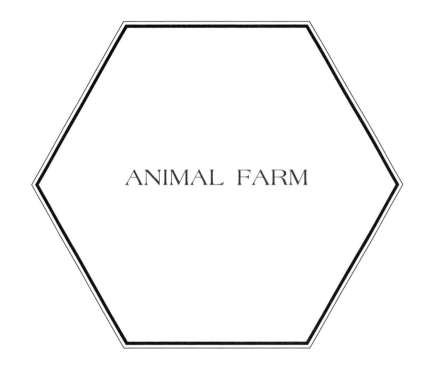

ANIMAL FARM

The Little Farmer Who Took a Stand

In Whatcom County, Washington, there labored a lowly but steadfast farmer who wished to raise some rather diminutive livestock: worms. At his Saber Tooth Worm Farm, Monte R. Littleton composted for his little herd an "ideal worm food" consisting of wheat straw, water, lime, soy meal, gypsum, and chicken droppings.

With apparently nothing better to do, the county health agency decided that concocting worm manna containing this last ingredient would necessitate Farmer Littleton's obtaining a solid waste handling permit. Farmer Littleton thought that the county health agency did not know its bureaucracy from chicken manure. So he sued the county agency in county court. He lost.

Farmer Littleton appealed to the Court of Appeals of Washington State. Proving once again that one person's trash is another's treasure, that learned tribunal ruled that solid waste does not include agricultural manures used for agricultural purposes. So Farmer Littleton's pride of worms is permitted to feast on their feast without a permit.

Moral:

Sometimes the small farmer just must take a stand
To enable his livestock to feed off the land,
And pray in its wisdom a high court affirms
The propriety of the Diet of Worms.

The Vet That Vented

Dr. Nelson had treated Lady for many years. Now Lady was old and sick, and Dr. Nelson kept telling Lady's owner, Betty, that it was time to put Lady to sleep. Betty, none too young herself at 76, vacillated. She made several appointments to have Lady euthanized, showed up, and then backed out.

Finally, one autumn day, Betty showed up again with Lady, and Dr. Nelson decided that he would act with dispatch to dispatch the dog. Unfortunately it took Dr. Nelson several attempts to inject the solution into Lady, which caused her to howl and collapse. Betty accused Dr. Nelson of killing Lady, which he had. She demanded that Dr. Nelson bring Lady back to life, which he did not.

Distressed, Betty filed a complaint against Dr. Nelson with the State Board of Veterinary Medicine. The Board sent an investigator to Dr. Nelson's office to investigate. Dr. Nelson did not mince words. He explained that Betty was a "******* wacko." With the investigator in his office, Dr. Nelson telephoned Betty to try to persuade her to drop the complaint. Betty was not persuaded. She accused Dr. Nelson of torturing and murdering her dog. Dr. Nelson barked back; he yelled at Betty that her soul would rot in hell for what she was trying to do to him.

It may not have helped Dr. Nelson's case before the Veterinary Board that he told them that he continued to pray every night that Betty rot in hell. Despite Dr. Nelson's evident piety, the Board found him guilty of professional incompetence. The Board ordered that he be publicly reprimanded. They also directed him to enroll in courses designed to help him communicate with the owners of animals entrusted to his care, although perhaps the problem was that he communicated all too clearly.

Dr. Nelson appealed to the Commonwealth Court, which agreed that while he had engaged in inexcusably rude conduct, that didn't amount to professional incompetence. In other words, while Dr. Nelson should have used other words, he could not be punished for not using other words.

Moral:

Although at times we all might pray
That certain clients rot in hell,
Remember, as your mom would say,
Not all you think is wise to tell.
But, if at clients you should swear,
For good or ill, the law won't care.

The Emotional State of Cows

The California Milk Producers Advisory Board ran a "Happy Cows" advertising campaign. Their slogan was, "Great cheese comes from happy cows. Happy cows come from California." An organization called the People for the Ethical Treatment of Animals was offended by the Happy Cows campaign, so offended that they sued the Milk Board under the California Unfair Business Practices Act. One can only surmise that PETA believed that California cows are not all that happy.

It is difficult to know exactly where the truth of the matter lies. At no point during the litigation were any cows called to the witness stand to testify on the subject. They uttered not a word.

The Milk Board was not cowed by PETA's lawsuit. You can't sue us, they said, even if California's cows are outright despondent, even suicidal. We're simply not covered by the Unfair Business Practices Act.

The California courts agreed with the Milk Board. We will not, said the courts, employ cow psychologists. We will not conduct an interstate survey of comparative cow composure. In short, the courts told PETA that its claim was the legal equivalent of cow manure.

Moral:

Courts will generally refrain
From struggling to ascertain
Just how some cow
Is feeling now.

The Squirrel Who Took On the Government

One fine day years ago in South Carolina, a little girl squirrel fell out of a tree. Fortunately she was discovered by a nice lady named Barbara who took her in, nursed her back to health, and named her Nutkin. Barbara and her husband built a room-sized enclosure for Nutkin to romp in, and life was good.

For reasons we know not, Barbara, her husband, and Nutkin moved to Pennsylvania, and there their legal woes began. Barbara's husband had occasion to call the Pennsylvania Game Commission to complain about a deer hunter poaching on their property. A Wildlife Officer came out to investigate. However, he really didn't care about deer poaching. Instead, the Wildlife Officer became upset when he spotted Nutkin frolicking in her enclosure. He informed Barbara that it was a violation of the law to keep such a wild animal. He threatened to issue a criminal citation unless Barbara relinquished Nutkin to his control, which she loyally refused to do.

As a result, the Wildlife Officer, as threatened, did issue Barbara a citation for the "unlawful taking or possession of wildlife." Barbara was duly

PLEASE LOOK OUT FOR THIS SQUIRREL

convicted of this crime by a district justice. She appealed and was again convicted by a trial judge, who imposed a sentence of a $100 fine plus court costs. Barbara appealed yet again from the trial court's decree.

The appellate court examined Nutkin's case with care and sympathy. Nutkin was by now well on in years, squirrel years anyway. It would be cruel, said the court, to turn her out into the world at her stage in life to fend for herself. It would be like sending an old appellate judge back to the boiling cauldron of the trial court after being tamed by years of peace and quiet above the fray.

Turning from whimsy to the law, the appellate court parsed the Pennsylvania statute prohibiting the unlawful taking and possession of wildlife, and found a loophole big enough to accommodate Nutkin. While it was true that it would have been unlawful to have taken Nutkin from the wild in Pennsylvania and domesticated her, such actions were lawful in South Carolina where they had occurred. Since Barbara had already possessed Nutkin legally before they came north, all was done in perfect harmony with Pennsylvania law. Thus did the appellate court quash Barbara's conviction for giving Nutkin a happy home. Barbara and Nutkin can live happily ever after, free of the tyranny of the Pennsylvania Game Commission.

Moral:
The Pennsylvania Game Commission
Was ill advised to hurl
The book at a "matrician"
Who saved an orphan squirrel.

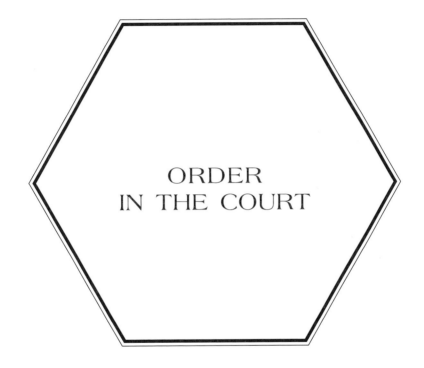

ORDER
IN THE COURT

Testamentary Trust

Not so very long ago in the venerable Commonwealth of Virginia, a condemned murderer named Michael Lenz raised various objections to the methods by which a jury of his peers determined his sentence. Michael's most inspired objection was that the jury was subjected to the extraneous influence of the Deity speaking through Holy Writ. Despite the findings of the circuit court that a juror had "at least one Bible and perhaps a 'Women's Devotional' with her in the jury room," that the Bible was open during the deliberations, and that one juror read from it and other jurors looked at it, the supreme court found no undue influence by the Supreme Being. Sentence affirmed: take it up directly with the Boss when you arrive at the Pearly Gates.

Moral:
A hanging jury is not liable
For taking guidance from the Bible.

Justice Delayed

Over the course of quite some time, in the hamlet of Ouachita, Louisiana, there sat a judge named Marcus Clark who, tragically, could not make up his mind. Although a statute mandated that judges judge within thirty days, Judge Clark often missed the mark, sometimes by as much as five years. Judge Clark worked long and hard, at times without even a law clerk to shepherd things along, but some cases were simply "lost" in the system because he didn't realize they were under advisement.

The highest court in that land thought and thought about how they could help Judge Clark speed things up. And what did they conclude? That Judge Clark must be suspended for thirty days from his judicial duties! Stand by. Stand by. Stand by.

Moral:
A judge whose cases aren't decided
Runs the risk of being chided.
And to ensure no more delay,
He's forced to take a holiday!

The Lawyer Who Wanted to Be Someone Else

Attorney A founded something called the Intermall Project, which became involved in a dispute with a group called Fairfield Communities. So, being a lawyer, Attorney A prepared a lawsuit on behalf of the Intermall Project against Fairfield. The only little thing was, he signed the complaint as Attorney B.

Fairfield hired Attorney C to represent it in the case. Attorney C contacted Attorney A (who he thought was Attorney B) to work out a settlement. They reached a deal the day before the case was scheduled to go to trial.

When Attorney A realized that he would have to present the settlement in court the next day, he panicked. Pretending to be B, he left a message for C saying that he (B) would be unable to appear in court but would send A in his stead. Things began to unravel when C met A and thought he sounded awfully like the lawyer known to him as B. His curiosity piqued, Attorney C called the real Attorney B who was quite surprised to learn that he had filed such a lawsuit.

Now Attorney C was really ticked, and told the judge on Attorney

A, who only made matters worse by denying to the judge what he had done. Of course, the truth finally came out.

At the disbarment proceedings, Attorney A finally 'fessed up. He offered all sorts of excuses for his little charade. And, he said, Attorney B would have filed the case if he had asked him.

Attorney A is no longer allowed to file lawsuits in anyone's name. Not even his own.

Moral:

Confronted with the bottom line
On documents that he must sign,
A lawyer would be daft should he go
And utilize an alter ego.

Too Guilty to Count

Wayne Prater was stopped by a police officer for driving his car with a broken taillight. The officer detected the smell of alcohol, went back to his cruiser, ran a check on Mr. Prater, and found that he had been arrested numerous times for driving under the influence. The officer informed Mr. Prater, who had exited his vehicle, that he was going to conduct a field sobriety test. Preferring broken field running, Mr. Prater legged it back to his car in an effort to effect his departure. The officer ran after him. When the officer tried to remove Mr. Prater from the driver's seat, Mr. Prater hit the gas and his vehicle hit the officer's leg, injuring it. Mr. Prater was later apprehended and charged with the crimes of driving while intoxicated and battery.

A jury of twelve of Mr. Prater's peers was impaneled to hear the case. Not surprisingly, they adjudged him guilty. As this was hardly the first time that Mr. Prater had engaged in antisocial misconduct, he was sentenced to five years hard labor.

Unhappy at this prospect, Mr. Prater took an appeal. The trial court, he argued, had overdone it. State law mandated that cases such as his were to be tried by a jury of six persons who must find him guilty. But here, twelve jurors had given him the proverbial thumbs down.

Rules are rules, said the appellate court. Since too many people found you guilty, the verdict must be overturned. You get a new trial and the chance to see if you can do any better with another six jurors. Of course, if the next six agree with the first twelve, that will be a valid conviction, even though the total would then be eighteen. Go figure!

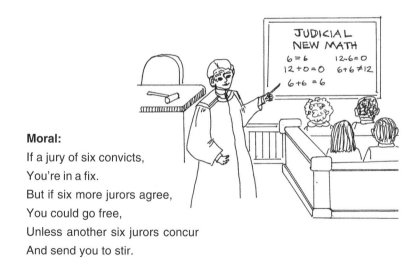

Moral:

If a jury of six convicts,

You're in a fix.

But if six more jurors agree,

You could go free,

Unless another six jurors concur

And send you to stir.

Striking Out

Although it may be hard to believe, many people do not particularly like lawyers. Donnell was one such person. In the middle of his trial on various criminal charges, including assault and murder, Donnell found himself unable to suppress his feelings any longer. He lashed out. Delicately phrased, he assaulted his own attorney.

No doubt feeling somewhat better, Donnell then argued that the judge who had observed this little outburst needed to take himself off the case. Donnell feared that the judge might be prejudiced against him, indeed might be inclined to believe that Donnell is the sort of fellow who commits antisocial acts. Unmoved, the judge said no.

Next, Donnell argued that he should be entitled to a delay in his trial as his new lawyer would need time to get up to speed on the case. (For some reason, his original lawyer had exited stage left.) Again the trial judge refused to accept this suggestion.

It will probably come as no surprise that the judge did find Donnell guilty on all counts.

Donnell appealed, claiming that he had been denied a fair trial. The Appellate Division did not sympathize. No matter what they might have privately thought of the first attorney, they concluded that it is not a good idea to let a criminal defendant gain a tactical advantage at trial by attacking his attorney to create a diversion. So, after Donnell struck out, he struck out.

Moral:

If during trial you feel the need
To rearrange your lawyer's face,
It may be fun, but your misdeed
Most likely won't assist your case.

The Juror
Who Was in a Hurry

Dwayne was to be tried by a jury of his peers on various criminal charges including assault and illegal weapons possession. The jury had been duly impaneled when Juror A suggested to Juror B that they could save themselves time and trouble by reaching a guilty verdict without bothering to hear the evidence. Juror B, a goody-two-shoes if ever there was one, promptly told the judge on Juror A. The judge questioned Juror A, who assured the judge that what he'd said had been in jest and that he would be delighted to sit through Dwayne's trial before determining his fate.

As it happened, after the trial had been tried, Juror A and Juror B and the other jurors on down the alphabet, all agreed that Dwayne was guilty as charged.

Dwayne appealed, claiming that it was a miscarriage of justice for Juror A to have remained on his case. But the appellate court affirmed Dwayne's convictions. Dwayne, they said, just had to learn how to take a joke.

Moral:

A jury should make some pretense

Of listening to the evidence,

But if they hurry,

Don't you worry

The courts will not take real offence.

The Flag That Was Too Grand

Hagan Smith went out fishing in his boat one fine summer's day near the Walnut Creek Marina. We do not know if he caught any fish, but when he docked his boat he himself got caught. Some Waterways Conservation Officers were conducting a routine boat safety inspection at the marina. A conservation officer issued Hagan a citation for violating the Fish and Boat Code by operating his boat without visible distress signals.

Visibly distressed, Hagan decided to fight his fine in court. And Hagan was as unwilling to pay a lawyer as he was to pay his fine. Not too surprisingly, the trial judge found him guilty of operating his boat without visible distress signals.

Hagan was still unwilling to cut bait, so he filed an appeal to the Pennsylvania Superior Court. Even though the Pennsylvania Superior Court didn't happen to be the right court for an appeal of a boating citation, the judges of that court figured that as long as Hagan was there they'd decide his case anyway. This wasn't too easy as, in his zeal to represent himself, Hagan had raised ninety-five points of contention. But, unlike Martin Luther's ninety-five theses, Hagan's ninety-five points didn't exactly catch on.

We will never know all of Hagan's ninety-five concerns, as the Pennsylvania Superior Court found most of them to be not worth mentioning. But his key complaint was that the American flag displayed in the trial court had a gold fringe. According to Hagan, a gold-fringed American flag represents martial or admiralty law, and therefore he didn't know what law applied to his case.

Although the appellate judges found this claim "bizarre," they dutifully reviewed federal and state flag laws to determine whether Hagan's rights had been infringed. They searched high and low and could find no statute supporting his position. They even unearthed an opinion of the Attorney General of the United States from the 1920s stating that you can display your flag with a fringe or without a fringe, and no one in the government will really care one way or the other. The judges concluded that Hagan's legal objection to the flag fringe was just one more fishing expedition on his part.

Moral:
If your courtroom flag is fringed,
There's no cause to become unhinged
And claim your rights have been impinged.

The Lawyer
Who Fought the Law

Montgomery Blair likes to sue people. Conveniently for him, he's also a lawyer. He used to be married to a woman named Barbara, but they haven't been married for a long time now. Nevertheless, Montgomery keeps suing Barbara, and the courts keep throwing out his lawsuits. He tried to take one of his domestic disputes all the way to the Supreme Court of the United States, but the Justices of that body decided that they had better things to do than to rehash Montgomery Blair's grievances against Barbara, so they refused to hear his case.

This frustrated Montgomery. It was wrong, he thought, for the Justices to deny him justice. So he did what he does best: he filed a lawsuit. This time he sued the United States Supreme Court and each Supreme Court Justice. He sought, among other remedies, one million dollars in damages from each individual Justice for — not to put too fine a point on it — treason.

The federal district court judge, whose decisions are ultimately subject to review by the United States Supreme Court, decided not to entertain the case and not to find his bosses' bosses guilty of treason and assess them a million bucks in damages.

Montgomery appealed to the federal circuit court of appeals, which, by the way, he had also sued. Those judges decided not to hear his appeal and not to enter a judgment against themselves either. This left him with only one recourse: asking the Justices of the Supreme Court to take the case against themselves. And did Montgomery really ask the Justices to decide whether they were guilty of treason and order themselves to pay him a cool million? You guessed it. Of course he did.

It hardly seems necessary to report whether the Justices agreed to hear Montgomery's appeal. We don't know if there was lengthy debate in the Court's chambers, but we do know the result. Once again, Montgomery's cries for justice against the Justices fell on deaf ears.

Moral:

If a lawyer who represents himself,
So it's said, has a fool for a client,
Then what can one say of a lawyer who sues
Every judge in a manner defiant?
I might say many things: just for starters
It's clear that his outlook for winning is gloomy.
I would like to say more, but I fear in this case,
If I did so, the lawyer would sue me.

The Defendant Who Was Accused of Signing His Name Too Many Times and Did Not Want It Used Again

Judicial Restraint

As you will certainly recall, in Shakespeare's Othello, the wicked Iago says, "he that filches from me my good name robs me of that which not enriches him, and makes me poor indeed."   Vincent Lafayette Lomax felt much the same way. He wanted no one but himself to use, or even speak, his name. While sitting in jail awaiting trial on three counts of passing bad checks, Vincent Lafayette Lomax filed various documents with the court in which he claimed to own his name by virtue of "common-law copyright of trade-name / trademark," whatever that may be. He decreed that anyone who used his name without his prior permission would be bound by a "self-executing contract / security agreement," whatever that may be, which provided that the "user" agreed to grant him a security interest in the user's assets in the amount of $500,000 for each unauthorized use.

When Vincent Lafayette Lomax was brought before Circuit Court Judge Donald E. Burrell, Judge Burrell was taking no chances. He asked Vincent to reconsider and allow him (the judge) to address him (Vincent) by name. Vincent politely but firmly refused. Judge Burrell threatened Vincent with criminal contempt, saying that Vincent's refusal to let the judge use his name in court would prevent him from trying the case. Vincent still refused; he argued that his name was his property and he had a constitutional right not to have his property used without compensation.

When further entreaty by Judge Burrell proved fruitless, he did indeed hold Vincent in contempt. Judge Burrell sent Vincent back to jail until he changed his mind.

Rather than relenting, Vincent filed a petition to the appellate court challenging Judge Burrell's contempt order. The appellate court cogitated over the matter and found that Vincent's refusal to let Judge Burrell use his name was not contemptuous. Vincent had at all times been civil to Judge Burrell and had never denied his identity. Cutting to the heart of the matter, the appellate court concluded that, notwithstanding Vincent's common-law copyright, trade-name, trademark, and self-executing contract / security agreement, the fact was that Judge Burrell simply didn't need Vincent's permission to use his name at trial. Thus Vincent's refusal to grant him permission didn't amount to a hill of beans, much less criminal contempt.

Moral:
Even if you should proclaim
That no one else can speak your name
(Of which you're no doubt rightly proud),
Still and all it is allowed.

WORKERS
OF THE WORLD

The Worker Who Worked to the Point of Exhaustion

Alfred worked for the Lockheed Martin Corporation for over twenty years and rose to the exalted rank of "production control processor." Not all those years were happy ones, at least not for Lockheed Martin. One evening when Alfred was "working" second shift, he was caught watching Monday Night Football, which, apparently, was not among the duties of a production control processor. He was written up for this disciplinary infraction and warned that any future misconduct could result in his discharge.

As you may already have guessed, Alfred did indeed reoffend. Some months after the Monday Night Football incident, Alfred was found asleep at a co-worker's desk during what Lockheed Martin believed to be his working hours. Lockheed Martin informed Alfred that his services were no longer required.

Alfred sued for unemployment compensation. Lockheed Martin said that sleeping on the job was disqualifying misconduct. The administrative law judge who heard the case agreed with Lockheed Martin and denied benefits. The Board of Review agreed with the administrative law judge. The Court of Appeals reversed.

In a learned opinion, the court reviewed the considerable juris-prudence concerning Americans falling asleep on the job. As appellate courts like to do, the Court of Appeal decided that a multifactor analysis needed to be undertaken. All those factors, said the court, aided Alfred. His job, they said, didn't really require him to be alert at all times. He wasn't sleeping in public. And, silly Lockheed Martin didn't have a written rule that employees not sleep on the job. At worst, said the court, poor Alfred "negligently took a nap." So Lockheed Martin now has to pay Alfred to sleep elsewhere.

Moral:

A negligent nap on the job is cool
As long as there's no written rule
And no one in the public sees
That you've stopped work to catch some zzzz,
On a job that doesn't take
Someone who is wide awake.

The Would-be Conductor

Like many a lad growing up, Andrew wanted to be a conductor. Not the kind with an orchestra, but the kind that runs a locomotive. He took and passed the qualifying exam for the New York City Transit Authority. Even so, his hopes were dashed, his plans derailed. The NYCTA decided to conduct its business without him.

Disappointed with the hiring process, Andrew turned to the courts for relief. It was, said he, a clear-cut case of discrimination. The NYCTA, said he, declined to hire him because he was an attractive male. Exactly why the NYCTA would not want attractive males in its employ, he did not explain. Nor can your reporter verify exactly how handsome Andrew was; his photo does not grace the court report.

Whether or not Andrew was the Adonis he thought himself to be, the court was not impressed. It will come as a blow to many of my readers that, in the court's view, attractive males do not constitute a recognized class protected by the law. Simply put, employers have the right to prefer to hire the homely. And that's the ugly truth.

Moral:

It's difficult to go through life

Accursed to be a handsome male;

And should this burden cause you strife,

The law will be of no avail.

The Cutup

In 1997, Kimberly took a job at the Costco store in West Springfield, Massachusetts. Back then when she was hired, she already had multiple earrings and four tattoos. Over the next few years she engaged in various forms of additional body modification, including facial piercing and cutting.

In 2001, Costco revised its dress code to prohibit all facial jewelry except earrings. Kimberly's supervisors told her that she would have to remove her facial piercings. But Kimberly came into work the next day still sporting a pierced eyebrow. Her supervisors were not mollified when she sanctimoniously explained that the various holes in her body were, literally, holy. She was, she said, a member of the Church of Body Modification.

According to its website, the Church of Body Modification was founded in 1999. Among the goals in its mission statement are for its members to grow as individuals through body modification and to be "confident role models in learning, teaching, and displaying body modification."

One of Kimberly's supervisors reviewed the information which she had provided from the Church's website, but was not converted. The supervisor told Kimberly again that she would have to remove her facial jewelry. Kimberly refused and filed a complaint of religious discrimination with the Equal Employment Opportunity Commission.

When Kimberly showed up for work the next day with her facial jewelry – but not her face – intact, she was sent home. Costco offered to let her return to work if she wore either plastic retainers or a band-aid over her jewelry. She rejected that offer because she believed that the Church's tenets required her to display all her facial piercings all the time.

The EEOC studied the sacred texts of the Church of Body Modification and concluded that Costco had indeed violated Kimberly's freedom of religion. Still Costco didn't see the light. So Kimberly sued Costco in federal court.

Although a trifle dubious about whether the Church of Body Modification is a bona fide religion, the federal judges decided not to decide that question. Rather, they concluded that it would be an undue hardship to require Costco to continue to employ a pinhead.

Moral:
If you believe that God decrees
That you must perforate your face,
You may learn that it doesn't please
Your boss who finds you a disgrace.
And courts won't help you out; instead
They'll think you've holes in your sweet head.

The Employee Who Didn't Want to Be a Trusty Friend

In the frozen northland known as Canada, a member of the Mi'kmaq tribe named Dorothy worked as a sales clerk at Play It Again Sports. During the year or so of Dorothy's employ, her bosses occasionally greeted her as "kemosabe." For the benefit of my younger readers who do not automatically associate Rossini's William Tell Overture with the American West and cowboys and Indians, the term "kemosabe" comes from the Lone Ranger movies and television shows of yesteryear.

When Dorothy asked her boss what "kemosabe" meant, he replied "my friend." She asked to be called by the Mi'kmaq word for friend, "nitap." But that didn't catch on with her bosses; they continued to call her kemosabe.

After Dorothy left her job at Play It Again Sports on bad terms, she filed a complaint of discrimination with the Nova Scotia Human Rights Commission. Although she raised various issues, the chief one was that her bosses had created a "poisoned work environment" by calling her kemosabe.

The kemosabe controversy was exhaustively explored at a hearing before a Board of Inquiry. Testimony was taken from expert linguists, one of whom performed a morphological analysis of the word "giimoosabe" derived from the Ojibwa or Potmowatmi language. Some members of the Memberton Band said they would be offended to be called "kemosabe," but others would not. One had never heard of the term; he was 19 years old.

Finding the conflicting testimony unedifying, the Board of Inquiry decided to go directly to the source. The Board, presumably at taxpayer expense, spent an entire day watching episodes from The Lone Ranger series. It will come as no surprise to my more mature readers that the Board concluded that the Lone Ranger was the star of the series and

Tonto was his partner and friend. The story line began when Tonto saved the Lone Ranger after the Texas Rangers had been ambushed by bad guys and Lone was the sole survivor. Tonto recognized Lone as the Ranger who had rescued him (Tonto) years earlier. Tonto called the Lone Ranger "kemosabe" and told him that it meant "trusty friend." Over the years and innumerable episodes, Tonto frequently called the Lone Ranger kemosabe and the Lone Ranger occasionally reciprocated.

Given the term's noble celluloid origin and honorific import, the Board had no choice but to find that "kemosabe" is not a racial slur. The Court of Appeals agreed, and Dorothy was left with not even so much as a silver bullet for her trouble.

Moral:

If your boss has got the hobby
Of calling you a kemosabe
And if you then walk off the job, he
Will not be in legal danger
For treating you like the Lone Ranger.

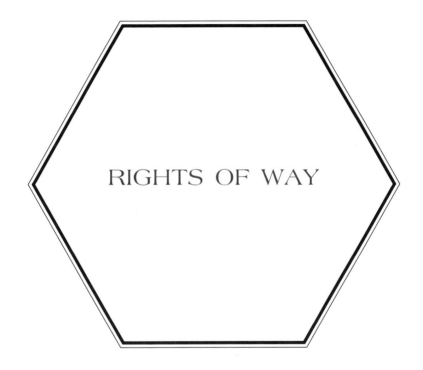

RIGHTS OF WAY

The Enterprising Entrepreneur Who Didn't Know the Difference

In the Great American Southwest, there was an enterprising entrepreneur named Renee who was the owner and operator of a tattoo and "body modification" establishment. One day, Renee published an advertisement offering free nipple piercing to any customer – male or female – on condition that the piercee have this delicate operation performed in the front window of the business. Knowing a good deal when they saw one, customers lined up. So did observers.

Unfortunately for Renee, one of those observers was a police officer. Being observant, he observed a female customer sitting in the store window exposing her frontal anatomy to the viewing public. Renee was busted.

A city ordinance forbade owners and operators of public places to permit or allow public nudity. The ordinance only applied to female breasts, not the male kind.

Renee reasoned that the ordinance violated equal rights by discriminating on account of sex. Based, no doubt, on years of study, the district court took judicial notice that the female breast is different from the male breast. Thus, the law can handle them differently.

Moral:
Justice, so it's said, is blind;
But surely even blind folks find
Differences in people's pecs
Associated with their sex.

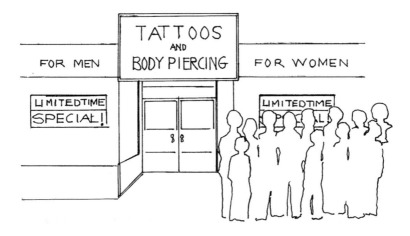

The Patriot and the Playing Cards

Like any patriotic American, Lawrence Saul was eager to show his support for our armed forces in time of national emergency. He did so on the streets of New York by selling decks of playing cards bearing photographic images associated with our (latest) war with Iraq. Failing to fully appreciate Saul's patriotism, the district attorney charged him with failure to obtain a general vendor's license.

Saul asked the court to dismiss the criminal complaint on the theory that the playing cards were "collectible war and military art created to memorialize Operation Iraqi Freedom and the Heroes of War." The court agreed that if the cards constituted a form of written or visual expression, they and their seller would be protected by the First Amendment and the general vendor's licensing scheme could not be applied.

Now, we all know that one person's art is another's kitsch is another's junk. Some prefer pictures of dogs playing poker, drinking beer, and smoking cigars; others, inexplicably, do not.

The court struggled with the rather abstruse question of what is, or is not, art. Should it apply Aristotelian logic based on deduction and investigation of the concrete, or favor a Platonic approach? No matter, said the court, art this is not. The photos are just, well, photos. And the words on the cards identifying the photos are just words; they have no expressive meaning.

But wait, said Saul, these are "collectibles." Yes, replied the court, but Webster's paradoxically tells us that a collectible is "a thing of no great intrinsic value." Why anyone would then collect collectibles, the court did not explain.

The bottom line, the court told Saul, is that if you want to be a war profiteer selling pictures of generals, you'll have to get a general vendor's license: the state must get its cut.

Moral:
'Tis aptly said that war is hell
And sometimes difficult to sell.

The Golfer
Who Got Exercised

Daniel Zurla didn't like the rules of the City of Daytona Beach's municipal golf courses which require golfers to use carts at certain times and on certain days. Following the exhortations of the Surgeon General and other health nuts, he just wanted to walk. No, said the city, in this sport you have to ride like everyone else.

We know not whether Mr. Zurla attempted to retain legal counsel and failed, or whether he simply decided to go it alone. In any event, representing himself, he sued the city, claiming that its cart-only rule violated his constitutional rights.

The learned judges in Florida scratched their collective heads. They were sure that they had studied the Constitution in law school and couldn't recall any provision regarding the right to walk on municipal golf courses. A fresh review of our nation's founding legal document confirmed their recollection. So they told Mr. Zurla to take a hike. But not on a municipal golf course during cart-only hours.

Moral:

Although fresh air and exercise
Are concepts many people prize,
If the city thwarts your goal
To take a healthy golfing stroll,
The law affords you no solution
Enshrined within the Constitution.

The Contestant
Who Lost Her Shirt

Vanessa entered the Miss Nude World International Pageant held at the celebrated Pink Pony, an adult entertainment club. Vanessa was already employed in the adult entertainment industry as a feature entertainer, meaning that she performed a "showgirl type Las Vegas review." She paid an entrance fee to be in the pageant and even hired a costume designer who created several costumes for her nude competition. (Exactly what type of costume one wears in a nude beauty pageant, your author cannot say.) Vanessa did well in the preliminary rounds, coming in as first runner-up in the voting in the "Gentlemen's Favorite" contest. As part of the competition, she then participated in a golf tournament, but refused to engage in a photo shoot on the links. She claimed that the photo shoot offended her delicate sensibilities.

One thing led to another. Rumors started flying that Vanessa had stuffed the ballot box in order to gain an advantage in the Gentlemen's Favorite contest. Despite her protestations of innocence, she was barred from the Pink Pony, thus ending her quest for the Miss Nude World International tiara. Her career as a nude entertainer lay in tatters.

So she sued everyone involved.

The jury, who could clearly see that she was otherwise unblemished, returned verdicts for Vanessa totaling almost a million dollars. Of course the defendants appealed.

On the first round of appeal, the appellate judges remanded the case to the trial court to supplement the record "with videotape evidence which had been shown to the jury but omitted from the record on appeal." The judges were naturally curious.

Apparently unimpressed by what they finally got to see on the videotape, the appellate judges eliminated all of Vanessa's damages except a paltry $3,500 for technical violations of the beauty pageant law. It was barely enough to cover her.

Moral:

A girl's own daddy should have told her
That beauty lies with the beholder.
She should not be a rotten loser
If pageant judges do not choose her;
And legal judges just won't care
That she has laid her assets bare.

The Dangers of Drink

In the Borough of Brooklyn, young Walker was enjoying a repast at a local eatery when a glass of water allegedly exploded in his hand. This allegation was alleged in the lawsuit brought by his mother on his behalf against the eatery's proprietors. Naturally, the proprietors asked the court to throw out the case. They argued that they were not in the "business of selling" the water or the water glasses they provide to their patrons.

The county court confronted the conundrum of whether a restaurant is in the business of selling the water and water glasses it provides at no charge to its parched patrons. The judge searched the learned tomes of New York law for precedent, but to no avail. With considerable pride, the judge reported that there were no decisions in New York State in which a party had even complained about the food in any of its myriad restaurants, let alone the utensils. This, said the judge, undoubtedly speaks well for the culinary emporia of the Empire State. But it didn't help him decide the matter. Accordingly, he searched for guidance beyond New York's borders.

Figuratively crossing the Hudson River, the judge found guidance in the Garden State of New Jersey. Diners, at least the thirsty ones, will be relieved to know that New Jersey has ruled that a restaurant impliedly warrants that the water it serves will be fit for human consumption. And, if the container that holds the water is defective, then the water is not fit to be consumed.

The New York judge agreed. Water glasses should hold water; the restaurant's defense did not.

Moral:

When you go out to have a bite
And lift your glass to quench your thirst,
The law says that you have the right
To know that glass won't up and burst.

Closely Watched Manes

The ladies who dance at Miss Sally's Gentlemen's Club were chafing. Not under their clothes, as they were wearing none. Rather they chafed against an ordinance of the City of Nyssa which prohibited nude entertainers at such establishments from entertaining within four feet of the nearest patron.

One evening a police officer entered Miss Sally's, presumably with a tape measure in hand, to size up the situation there. The officer observed a nude dancer shaking her hair in a patron's face. Less than a foot separated the patron from the lady's locks. No doubt concerned about possible transmissions of head lice, the officer arrested the owners and managers of Miss Sally's.

The defendants were convicted in the Nyssa Municipal Court of violating the four-foot barrier. They appealed to the County Court, and lost. They appealed to the Court of Appeals, and lost. They finally appealed to the Supreme Court of Oregon.

They argued to the high court justices that the ordinance violated the right of free expression guaranteed by the Oregon Constitution. Their dancers were merely trying to express themselves in the most direct fashion possible to the patrons who likewise surely wanted to closely examine those expressions.

Although it seems certain that the patrons paid to peruse the performers and that the dancers in turn received some form of recompense for their exertions, the Oregon Supreme Court concluded that the ordinance did violate the right to free expression. Ergo, the owners and managers of Miss Sally's were freed of their convictions. And their dancers were free to return to their daily grind.

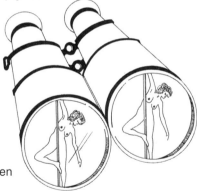

Moral:

A town can't keep a dancing queen
Who wishes to be clearly seen
From getting in a patron's face
So he can judge her style and grace.

The Coed
Who Was Up a Tree

Elizabeth was a student at Cornell University. One chilly windy November day, she decided to climb a hickory tree on campus and seat herself up there. We do not know why, but she did. She secured herself to the hickory with a safety line and sat upon a platform tied to the tree with ropes.

University Police Officer Stanley came upon the scene and ordered Elizabeth down. For your own safety, he said. Trees are unpredictable, he said. Elizabeth demurred, and Officer Stanley called for backup. Soon Jane, the University Events Manager, joined Officer Stanley. Jane attempted to manage the event by reading Elizabeth a formal statement that she (Elizabeth) was in violation of University rules and regulations, and that if she (Elizabeth) did not forthwith cease and desist, the University would press charges against her. Nonetheless, Elizabeth stayed perched in her perch for the rest of the afternoon. As evening descended, so did she.

True to its threat, Cornell University went to the authorities and had Elizabeth charged with trespass and disorderly conduct.

The City Court of Ithaca examined the situation. The judge noted that Cornell's Campus Code of Conduct, while addressing many meaty matters, is strangely silent on the subject of tree-sitting. The judge opined that tree-sitting has a noble history as a means of expressing protest. Whatever Elizabeth may have been protesting, she had the right to do so. As long as she hadn't interfered with Cornell's teaching and research missions, which she hadn't, Elizabeth wasn't guilty of trespass.

Likewise, since Elizabeth hadn't inconvenienced the public, her conduct, while perhaps not exactly orderly, wasn't disorderly either.

In short, when it prosecuted Elizabeth, Cornell was barking up the wrong tree.

Moral:
When we were young, guys went to college
Relentlessly pursuing knowledge,
Interspersed with chugging beer
And raiding coeds' underwear.
If kids today should go tree-sitting,
Who's to say it's not befitting?

ALL IN THE FAMILY

The Boy Who Was Saved by a Weatherman and the Law

Marlene had a baby boy. She filed a paternity action against the weatherman at a local television station. All the little genes pointed to the weatherman, and he was duly determined to be the daddy. The weatherman then sued for custody of his son, and won. He also asked the court to change the lad's name to Samuel Charles, on account of the mom had named him "Weather'By Dot Com Chanel Fourcast."

Why? asked the judge. Why did you name a little baby, too young to defend itself, Weather'By Dot Com Chanel Fourcast? (Here, your scrivener must confess a little difficulty in explaining the explanation, but will try his best.) It was Weather'By because Mom had always heard of Weatherby as a last name, Dot Com because she'd worked on a teleprompter computer and she thought it was "kind of cute," Chanel for the perfume and because she'd heard of a "black little girl named Shanel," and Fourcast – instead of forecast – for her fourth child.

Without impugning the Mom's motives or imagination, the judge ruled that a name change to Samuel Charles was in Weather'By Dot Com Chanel Fourcast's best interest. The Court of Appeals found Mom's appeal unappealing, and affirmed.

Moral:

Although a rose by any name would smell as sweet,
Any kid on the playground would be dead meat
Whose clever but misguided mother hast
Dubbed him Weather'By Dot Com Chanel Fourcast.
And so we applaud the kind judge who did
Save the poor hide of one little kid.

The Father Who Was Too Honest with His Sons

There once was a father whose twin sons grew up to make it big, first directing music videos, then producing motion pictures. No doubt, dad's bosom swelled with pride. Apparently the feeling was not mutual.

One son gave an interview which was published in a well-known magazine in which he claimed, "Our dad's a pimp." In another published interview, his twin elaborated that dear old dad "dabbled in the pimptorial arts."

His feelings understandably hurt, dad sued his sons for defamation, claiming that they had besmirched his high honor and sullied his reputation. At trial, the twins produced evidence that when they were little, their daddy told them that at one time he had been a person who lived off the illicit earnings of women who were paid for dispensing their favors. The twins did not, however, demonstrate that dad still engaged in such endeavors. Nevertheless, the jury returned a verdict for the twins on the basis that truth is a defense to defamation.

Dad appealed on a lot of grounds, but the key one was that even if he used to be a pimp, it did not follow that it's true that he still is a pimp.

The Court of Appeal cogitated deeply on what it means to be a pimp. The judges surely delved into many books on the subject. Finally they decided to go with the old adage, "Once a pimp, always a pimp."

It looks like dad won't be getting a share of those movie profits after all.

Moral:

Doting parent, my advice is:
Never tell your little kids
That you once engaged in vices
Of the sort the law forbids.

The Dad Who
Tried to Trade His Truck

Jerald had two problems to get rid of: an $89-a-week child support payment to Pamela and a ten-year-old pickup truck. One can almost see the wheels turning his head. "Pam," he said, "what say I give you the pickup truck and you forgive me three years' worth of child support?"

Pam, who no doubt had heard pickup lines before, was somewhat wary. Jerald explained that he had talked to someone at the state who told him he couldn't make a direct trade. So he and Pam signed an agreement that Jerald was selling her the truck for $90 a week for 156 weeks and they would trade receipts each week (child support vs. truck payments) rather than money.

Like the truck itself, the whole scheme broke down. Pam wasn't able to register the truck because there was a lien recorded against it and Jerald wouldn't present papers to show that the lien was discharged. Pam and Jerald couldn't agree on signing future support receipts. Meanwhile the truck sat unregistered in Pam's driveway, not doing her or Jerald or their child any good. And, of course, Jerald stopped paying child support.

Pam sued Jerald for past-due child support and got a ruling that Jerald owed her $13,000. Jerald sued Pam for breach of contract, and got a ruling that Pam owed him $14,000, which she had to either pay him directly or credit against his child support. Pam appealed.

The appellate court found that there was a contract for sale of the truck, but it was against public policy to tie it to child support. Pam and Jerald couldn't bargain away the child's right to support, and the trial court was wrong to credit Jerald for unpaid child support in exchange for the truck.

Moral:

If one fine day you make a kid
And now must pay 'cause you're a father;
A traded truck will not get rid
Of child support; so do not bother.

The Party at Grandma's and Who Was to Blame

Leanna had been quite a naughty girl, in trouble with the authorities, the subject of numerous juvenile proceedings. You get the picture. At the age of seventeen, she showed up one day at her grandmother's house in California, having run away from her most recent juvenile placement.

Delighted to see her descendant, Grandma promptly bought Leanna a one-way bus ticket to Montana, where Leanna's mom lived. Grandma's first mistake was that she bought the ticket on a Friday, but Leanna was not supposed to leave until the following Monday. Grandma's second mistake was going away for the weekend. Grandma told Leanna that she would have to stay elsewhere until Sunday evening. Grandma locked up her house tight. But not tight enough.

After Grandma left on Friday, Leanna persuaded the somewhat naive next-door neighbor to loan her a key to Grandma's house to pick up her luggage for the trip. Leanna had decided to throw herself a going-away party, and she'd invited some thirty or forty of her intimate friends to join in. By the time the dust settled on Sunday, Grandma's house was not exactly in the pristine condition in which she'd left it. In

fact, the place was pretty well trashed. Among the missing were cash, jewelry, a cell phone, and six bottles of booze. Also, the Direct TV bill for the weekend included a $110 fee for a boxing match and six "adult" movies.

As a result, Leanna was adjudicated in juvenile court to have committed burglary and vandalism. She appealed, and won.

The Court of Appeals reasoned that to commit burglary, someone must enter unlawfully with the intent to commit a theft or any felony. Unlawfully enter, she did. But what was Leanna's intent at the time she entered? The court had no answer to this rather metaphysical question. Perhaps she'd planned to polish the silver. Anyhow, no one – except Leanna's party pals, who were understandably reticent on the subject – could say who actually took the loot and trashed the joint.

Without evidence that little Leanna had entered intending to be a bad girl and that it was she who did the dirty deeds, she walked on the burglary charge. Ditto vandalism.

Even though Leanna was cleared by the courts, it is unclear how thrilled her mom will be to provide her with another place to crash.

Moral:
When you break into Grandma's pad,
Be smart and bring your friends along;
Then if the party turns out bad,
The law can't prove just who did wrong.

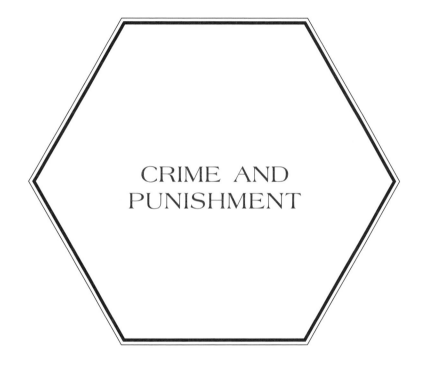

CRIME AND
PUNISHMENT

What the Wiccan Wanted

When the moon would get full in sunny Florida, all Lynn Austin wanted to do was go outside for private Esbat celebratory rituals, pursuant to her Wiccan faith. But the warden concluded that letting inmates out at night on a regular basis might not be a very bright idea. So Austin brought a lawsuit to establish her First Amendment right to "draw down the moon."

Florida's judges, not being themselves lunatics, rather thought not. Austin will need to dig up another way to get out of jail.

Moral:
A warden would have to be more than jejune
To let inmates out to go bay at the moon.

The Defendant Who Seized His Opportunity and Was, in Turn, Seized

In the City of New York, there lived a certain Mr. Spalding who had occasion to visit the office of his local public defenders organization. We do not know what prior indiscretions may have occasioned that visit. After Mr. Spalding had bidden his farewells, an employee of the public defenders noticed that not only had Mr. Spalding departed, but so had her small brown Fendi handbag. Bereft, she notified the authorities.

Shortly thereafter, the ill-advised Mr. Spalding attempted to reenter the Criminal Court Building carrying a knapsack. He approached an Officer McGonnigle who was manning a Magnetometer Station at the front entrance to the Courthouse. (Connecting the dots, one may suppose that the same unfortunate matters that had earlier brought Mr. Spalding to the public defenders office prompted his subsequent calling upon the Criminal Court.)

Like an airplane passenger, Mr. Spalding was required to place the contents of his pockets in a plastic bin and hand his knapsack to Officer McGonnigle to be run through the "mag" to be x-rayed. The x-ray showed clusters of items inside the knapsack which, upon Officer McGonnigle's inspection, included – surprise, surprise – a Fendi purse. Mr. Spalding gallantly explained that "I found it in the courtroom and I was bringing it back." Unfortunately this noble stated purpose was belied by Officer McGonnigle's finding the public defenders' employee's checkbook elsewhere in the knapsack and her driver's license and debit card secreted inside Mr. Spalding's wallet.

Despite Mr. Spalding's later protestations that his right to be free from unreasonable search and seizure had been violated, the court concluded that one must expect to be inspected when entering a courthouse in these explosive times. Thus Mr. Spalding ended up with further felonies.

Moral:

You know a heist has been ill planned
When the heister smuggles contraband
By a most circuitous route
Into a court, instead of out.

A Close Brush with the Law

Duke and Jerry Board, the Board Brothers, got themselves arrested on murder charges on August 2, 2000. The Brothers spent one hundred and twenty-six days locked up in the Edgar County Jail before they were acquitted and sent home to their kith and kin.

Not satisfied with their vindication in criminal court, and not having had enough of the legal system, the Brothers turned around and sued their former hosts, their jailers and the county sheriff, in federal court. The Brothers claimed that they had been subjected to inhumane conditions in jail which infringed their constitutional rights. They had a variety of complaints. In what is destined to be known someday as "Colgategate," Brother Duke alleged that he had been deprived of toothpaste for over three weeks.

The sheriff and the jailers asked the court to throw the case out. They had no way of knowing, said they, that there's a constitutional right to toothpaste.

But in an incisive opinion filled with wisdom, the United States Court of Appeals ruled that such a deprivation is not a proper way to take a bite out of crime.

Moral:

Those who may have caused a death
Retain the right to minty breath.

The Booty That Brought Down the Bandit

Robert went to the supermarket with what must have seemed like a foolproof plan. He wore two pairs of pants, one inside the other. The inner pair had elastic at the ankles. As Robert went along pilfering products, he slipped them inside his pants.

When the day manager came on shift, a store employee called to his attention a customer who was walking strangely, as if both of his legs were broken. It was Robert, walking quickly but awkwardly toward the exit. Robert did not stop at the cash register to perfect any purchases, and an alarm went off indicating that he had taken unpaid for merchandise with him.

Robert looked back and saw the manager giving chase, so he tried to run for it. But he was done in by his product selection. He made loud noises as he ran, and liquid began to run down his legs. He fell, got up, but was tackled by the manager and a security guard. When the police arrived, they counted six broken and three intact bottles of booze in Robert's pants. And, to add injury to insult, the broken bottles had cut his ankles. The bottles, one might say, were his Achilles' heels.

Although Robert's attorneys diligently tried to explain to the court that there was a perfectly innocent explanation for Robert's behavior, he was duly convicted of theft of goods and sent to a place where the state will provide him with one pair of pants at a time.

Moral:

When filching goods, don't take the chance
Of stuffing bottles down your pants,
Because if you are seen and chased,
They'll slow you down and go to waste.
So, as you choose which goods to lift,
Recall the race goes to the swift.

A Legal Flip Flop

One summer evening, in our Nation's Capital, there erupted a neighborhood squabble. Virginia (a woman, not the Commonwealth of) and Javett exchanged heated words. Getting ready for battle, Virginia removed her earrings and flip flops, and closed on Javett. At some stage during the ensuing altercation, Virginia retrieved a flip flop and popped Javett a good one in the face with it, causing a cut that required fifteen stitches to repair.

The law was called in. Virginia was arrested, tried, and convicted of simple assault and attempted possession of a prohibited weapon. Virginia appealed.

The appellate court agreed that Virginia had assaulted Javett. After all, she had.

The real issue on appeal was whether the offending flip flop was a prohibited weapon. Virginia's ace attorney argued that, under the law, for a flip flop to be a prohibited weapon it had to be likely to produce death or great bodily injury as it was used. The flip flop in question was of the flat, rubber-soled variety.

The appellate court concluded that Virginia was lucky to manage to break her victim's skin with such a flip flop and could not have really expected to induce serious injury or death with it. Refusing to waffle on the issue, the court reversed the flip flop as prohibited weapon conviction.

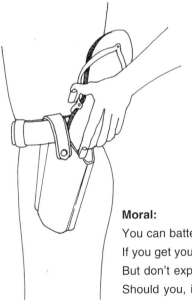

Moral:
You can batter someone with a flip flop
If you get yourself counsel that's tip top...
But don't expect to win appeals
Should you, instead, employ high heels.

Double Jeopardy

Travis Lee Gibson is a very bad man indeed, not the sort of fellow you'd want to cross, or even, for that matter, meet. One dark night, Travis and some fellow miscreants broke into a house shared by Joshua and Steve. Travis and his gang wanted to rob Joshua and Steve, but when that didn't work out, they decided to shoot them instead. Travis shot both Joshua and Steve. Steve survived; Joshua didn't.

Travis and pals decided it was a good time to leave town. But Travis, who apparently is dumb as well as mean, returned and was soon arrested for his various misdeeds. A jury duly convicted Travis of aggravated murder, felony murder, and a bunch of other crimes. Feeling that Travis would not be mourned, the judge imposed not one, but two, sentences of death.

Shocked, Travis appealed, raising thirty four assignments of error. By and large, the appellate court was not impressed by most of his arguments. But the appellate judges did agree that his double death sentence was overly harsh, given that he had managed, despite his best efforts, to murder just one victim. So, dispensing mercy with justice, they halved his sentence and decreed that Travis need only be executed once.

Moral:

Although learned judges
Cut his sentence in half,
A twice-condemned killer
Won't enjoy the last laugh.

"I hear his lawyer got his sentence cut in half."

The Bartender Who Should Have Been More Observant

Karen was a bartender at Jack's Bar and Grill in the town of Good Thunder in the county of Blue Earth in the state of Minnesota. The Blue Earth County Sheriff's Office was concerned about an ongoing problem of minors consuming alcohol, which apparently did not leave sufficient quantities for the adult members of the community. More specifically, Jack's Bar and Grill was known to the Blue Earth County Sheriff's Office as a problem spot, having failed at least two compliance checks.

Although the Blue Earth County Sheriff's Office had no particular beef with Karen, they decided to send a minor into Jack's Bar and Grill to see if he'd be served. They provided a nineteen-year-old with a $20 bill, wired him with audio-surveillance equipment, and directed him to try to buy some booze. They said that if the bartender requested, he should produce an ID showing his true age.

Cleverly disguised with a khaki cap, the tender lad entered Jack's B & G, purposefully strode up to the bar, and asked Karen the bartender

for a twelve-pack of beer. Karen tendered the beer; he tendered the $20 and left bearing the beer.

The Blue Earth County Sheriff's Office swooped down on the unsuspecting Karen and charged her with providing alcoholic beverages to a minor.

It's unfair, Karen protested; the niceties of due process were not observed. That sneaky Blue Earth County Sheriff's Office should not have used a sneaky underage purchaser to prove an underage purchase. I was tricked, hoodwinked.

Sadly for Karen, the courts did not agree that the Blue Earth County Sheriff's Office had used deceptive or overbearing means to obtain a conviction. It's your own fault, the courts told Karen. You should have paused a moment in your haste to slake the public's thirst and taken the time to read the inscription on the lad's cap, which proudly proclaimed: "Blue Earth County Sheriff's Office Alcohol Compliance Team."

Moral:
Bartenders, as a group, are wise,
Dispensing wisdom to the guys.
But one would have been a great deal wiser
Had she bothered to read a patron's visor.

HOLIDAY STORIES

Unexpected Fireworks

Two friendly neighbors resided side by side in the town of Framingham, Massachusetts. Prior to leaving on vacation, Neighbor Carl asked Neighbor William to water Carl's flowers while he (Carl) was away. Neighbor William agreed. Neighbor Carl vacated. On the Fourth of July, Neighbor William went to Carl's house, took a hold of his garden hose and grabbed the outside faucet. Fireworks ensued. The electric shock he received threw William many feet into the air, melted his sneakers and glasses, set his pants on fire and knocked his dental plate from his mouth. When the fire department arrived, they found water in Carl's basement. The source of the water was a second-floor toilet, which, although he later denied it, Carl had apparently attempted to repair himself, as homeowners are sometimes wont to do.

William sued Carl. William lost. Finding no "proximate cause," the court opined that while one could envision a variety of foreseeable injuries arising out of a defective second floor toilet, an electric shock to a neighbor when he touches a faucet outside the house is not one of them.

Moral:

The homeowner who tries to repair his own toilet

Likely as not is going to spoil it;

And the neighbor who offers his flowers to water

Will be as the lamb who is led to the slaughter.

The Lady
Who Was Amazed

One evening, Mrs. Durmon accompanied the church youth group on a Halloween visit to a local cornfield that had been transformed into three maize mazes. She paid what we assume was perfectly good money to go into the first, short and easy, maze, and even more money for the second maze which was longer, more difficult, and "haunted."

As Mrs. Durmon wended her way through the first maze, she realized that the ground was muddy (not too unusual for a field in the fall) and she heard the sound of a chainsaw emanating from the haunted maze (not too unusual for scaring the bejesus out of people). She completed the first maze without untoward incident and proceeded into maze two. Disaster struck.

A man dressed as Jason from the movie Friday the Thirteenth, complete with orange jumpsuit and hockey mask, approached Mrs. Durmon holding a running chainsaw (from which the chain had been removed) over his head. Mrs. Durmon was scared. She turned, tried to run, fell, and broke her ankle.

Mrs. Durmon went to the doctors to fix her ankle. Then she went to

the lawyers to fix the people who ran the maze. Her lawyers sued. They argued that the maze managers were negligent because the ground was muddy and also because they didn't adequately warn visitors that they might be frightened in the haunted maze.

The court could not agree that the maze masters had been negligent. They didn't make the cornfield muddy, and Mrs. Durmon knew from the first maze that it was muddy. And the haunted maze was supposed to be scary. That was the whole point.

Aw shucks, Mrs. Durmon couldn't collect from the maize maze for her ankle anguish.

Moral:

Both you and the law should be undaunted
If you're scared at events which you know to be haunted.

Ho Ho Ho

Darron Murphy Sr. was found guilty by a federal jury of tampering with a witness who was going to testify against his son in another case, using a firearm while doing the tampering, and various and sundry related misdeeds. He appealed his convictions to the United States Court of Appeals for the Seventh Circuit.

Three learned federal appeals judges raked their way through the official transcript prepared by the trial court reporter to glean the facts and search for any errors. According to the official transcript, Murphy Sr. had called the prospective witness a "snitch bitch hoe" before smacking her in the head.

The ever-alert appellate judges instantly realized that a serious mistake had in fact been made, but by the court reporter rather than by the jury or trial judge. A "hoe," the judges patiently explained, is a tool used for weeding or gardening. In context, it did not seem that Murphy Sr. would have called his victim a garden tool.

Rather, the appellate judges suggested that Murphy Sr. must be a rap music fan and intended to call his victim a "ho" in the sense used by the rapper Ludacris when he so beautifully raps, "You doin' ho activities with ho tendencies." Sticklers for detail, the appellate judges changed the spelling of "hoe" to "ho." But Murphy Sr. did not get the last laugh; they also upheld his convictions.

Moral:

Court reporters now must know
The difference 'twixt a "hoe" and "ho."

The Gambler
and the Garland

It was the eve of Christmas Eve, and Martina and her family were in a celebratory mood. So, in lieu of going to services, they decided to get into the spirit of the season by playing the slot machines at the Isle of Capri Casino.

A festive mood prevailed at the casino; it was all decked out for Christmas. Muzak carols no doubt filled the air.

The slots were located on the second floor. Perhaps in anticipation of festive feasts, Martina and her family chose to take the stairs. Even the staircase was decorated for the holidays, with garlands and bows draped from the banister. And there, allegedly, lay the problem.

As Martina began her ascent up the stairs, it precipitously turned into a rapid descent. She tripped, possibly over an errant garland that was hanging down on the stairs. She reached for the railing, but only grabbed a garland instead, which came off in her hand. And down she went.

Apparently Martina was not so severely injured as to impede her ability to continue on up to the second floor and play the slots. We do not

know how she did with the one-armed bandits that night, but we do know how she fared in the ensuing litigation.

Three years after her run-in with the Christmas decorations, Martina sued the casino owners, claiming that she had been seriously injured.

The case went to trial, and at the close of testimony the trial judge ruled in favor of the casino. So Martina sought redress from a higher authority.

The Court of Appeals religiously reviewed the record. One can just imagine the appellate judges asking themselves if they really wanted to go down in history as the Grinches who told business establishments that they can't put up Christmas decorations. Clearly they did not.

Turning to the legal issues at hand, the appeals court questioned whether Christmas garlands are inherently dangerous materials. No, said the three wise men of the court, they are not really like other items we've found in the past to be inherently dangerous, such as dynamite or unexploded antiaircraft shells. Finally, said they, there was no negligence, for surely the garlands were hung by the banister with care, in hopes that St. Nicholas—or gullible gamblers—soon would be there.

Moral:
If you're felled by a holiday railing,
Litigation will be unavailing.
So, then, here's my advice:
Whether naughty or nice,
You'd be better off going wassailing.

Legal Citations

Boldface numbers refer to the page on which the corresponding fable begins.

72 Commonwealth v. Smith, 868 A.2d 1253 (Pa. Super. 2005).

74 Sibley v. United States Supreme Court, 136 Fed. Appx. 252 (11th Cir. 2005), cert. denied, 126 S.Ct. 666 (2005).

76 Lomax v. Merritt, 153 S.W.3d 904 (Mo. App. S.D. 2005).

80 Brandon v. Lockheed Martin Corp., 872 So.2d 1232 (La. App. 4 Cir. 2004).

82 Blitzer v. New York City Transit Authority, 784 N.Y.S.2d 528 (A.D. 1 Dept. 2004).

84 Cloutier v. Costco Wholesale Corp. 390 F.3d 126 (1st Cir. 2004).

86 Nova Scotia Human Rights Commission v. Play It Again Sports Ltd., [2004] N.S.J. No.403, 2004 NS.C. Lexis 448.

90 City of Albuquerque v. Sachs, 92 P.3d 24 (N.M. App. 2004).

92 People v. Saul, 776 N.Y.S.2d 189 (N.Y. City Crim. Ct. 2004).

94 Zurla v. City of Daytona Beach, 876 So.2d 34 (Fla. App. 5 Dist. 2004).

96 Galardi v. Steele-Inman, 597 S.E.2d 571 (Ga. App. 2004).

98 Gunning v. Small Feast Caterers, 777 N.Y.S.2d 268 (Sup. 2004).

100 City of Nyssa v. Dufloth, 121 P.3d 639 (Or. 2005).

102 People v. Millhollen, 786 N.Y.S. 2d 703 (City Ct. 2004).